HE REMEMBERED TO SAY THANK YOU

Luke 17:11-19 FOR CHILDREN

Written by Victor Mann

Illustrated by Betty Wind

ARCH® Books

COPYRIGHT © 1976 CONCORDIA PUBLISHING HOUSE, ST. LOUIS, MISSOURI

MANUFACTURED IN THE UNITED STATES OF AMERICA

ALL RIGHTS RESERVED

ISBN 0-570-06103-2

In a little town on the top of a hill,
At the end of a narrow street,
A kind old priest with tears in his eyes
Wiped the dust from his tired feet.

He sat with Hiram and stared at the ground.
The words were hard to say.
"Hiram," he said, "I have very sad news.
You must leave this town right away.

"You have a disease called leprosy.
I wish it were not true.
But you must go so your family and friends
Don't get the sickness from you.

"No one should ever come close to you.
So if you should meet a stranger,
Cry out very loudly, 'Unclean! Stay away!'
To warn him about the danger."

Hiram left town. He felt hurt and alone
When everyone called him "unclean."
He wanted to say good-bye to his friends,
But they were afraid to be seen.

They hid behind stairways, peeked around
    doors,
And climbed up the tallest trees.
They were so frightened they stayed far away
From their friend with the dreaded disease.

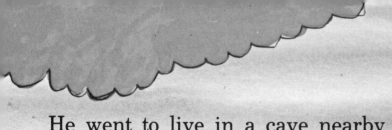

He went to live in a cave nearby
That he and his friends had found.
When they had come to play there together,
The cave had a cheerful sound.

He leaned against a sycamore tree
And looked at the clear blue sky.
He wanted to dance and sing again.
Instead he started to cry.

Tears trickled down his thin, pale cheeks
As he prayed, "God, let me be free.
I'll thank You and serve You every day
If you'll cure my leprosy."

For many years Hiram lived alone.
Then very late one night
Nine more lepers came with such wonderful news
It made Hiram dance with delight.

"Jesus is coming this way tomorrow.
We've come to see Him," they said.
"He must have the power to heal leprosy.
He brought people back from the dead."

Hiram kept dancing and
shouting for joy.
His happiness spilled
everywhere.

Jesus was coming
        the very next day.
God had answered
        his prayer.

He tossed and turned in his bed all night.
He was much too excited to rest.
What would he say when Jesus came?
Would Jesus hear his request?

Long before the sun came up,
When the air was very still,
He got up quickly and left the cave
And climbed to the top of the hill.

He waited and watched the road for hours.
His body began to ache.
He closed his eyes and nodded his head.
He couldn't stay awake.

The sun was low in the orange sky
When Hiram awoke with a start.
He jumped to his feet and looked around.
Fear filled his pounding heart.

"I missed Him," Hiram cried to himself.
"Something always goes wrong.
How could I miss my chance to be healed?
Why did I sleep so long?"

Then far away he heard the sound
Of a noisy, laughing crowd.
He saw the dust from their tramping feet
Rise in a swirling cloud.

He rubbed his eyes and shook his head
To be sure it wasn't a dream.
A happy cheer got stuck in his throat
Then escaped in a squeaky scream.

The lepers all ran down the hill.
"We're tired of being alone.
Jesus, Master, have mercy on us.
Please heal us so we can go home."

A hush fell over the startled crowd.
Fear danced in their terrified eyes.
They began to shout, "Keep away from us."
But Jesus silenced their cries.

He turned to the men, who were still far away,
And called out across the field,
"Go into the village and find the priest
To show him that you have been healed."

The countryside rang with happy shouts
As the ten men rushed to the priest.
They couldn't wait to be welcomed home
With a party, or maybe a feast.

But suddenly Hiram stopped and remembered
The promise he made in his prayers.

He ran back and said, "I thank you, Lord,
For showing me how much God cares."

Jesus was silent, then asked the crowd,
"Where are the other men?
Why has only one man returned
When God's gift was given to ten?"

"Of all those men only this one remembered
To thank God for what he received.
Go home to your friends," Jesus said to Hiram.
"You are well because you believed."

DEAR PARENTS:

Hiram the leper is the perfect image of each of us as sinner. Hiram was isolated from his community and forced to see himself as not-OK. Have your child point out to you how ugly and lonely leprosy made Hiram feel, e. g., people hid from him, shouted at him, he cried, etc.

Be sure to explain, however, that having any disease — including leprosy — is in no way a mark of being sinful. Disease is a result of sin in the world, but not a punishment for an individual person's sins — Jesus' miracles of healing show us how happy and whole God wants all of us to be.

Just as Hiram's leprosy separates him from other people, so his healing comes with a crowd, first the other lepers, then Jesus and his followers. Christianity always means people. Jesus makes Hiram and the other lepers OK by having them go back to their community — to their priest. And the healed lepers expect to have a party to celebrate their return.

The result of being made to feel really OK by Jesus is Hiram's ability to say thank you. When we know we are OK through Jesus, we acknowledge our need for help and can help others. We open up. Hiram was doubly healed: He looked better and he felt better.

Let your child describe his/her own feelings of not being OK and subsequent feelings of ugliness and loneliness. Then help him/her realize Jesus' OK that permits us to love and affirm others. A kiss and hug would be an appropriate way to conclude.

THE EDITOR